92
LEO
RIPLEY, ELIZABETH
Leonardo da Vinci

1261

DATE DUE			
FEB 25	MAY 27	MAR 27	1996
APR 1	JUN	FEB 20	
NOV 16		NO 26 '02	
JAN 11		DE 15 '06	
JUN 18		DE 19 06	
APR 8			
MAR 31	FEB 26		
MY 24			
OCT 2	MR 15 1995		
OCT 29	MR 28 1995		
GAYLORD M-2	MR 28 1995	PRINTED IN U.S.A.	
	MAR 07 1996		

92
Leo   *Ripley 1261*

LEONARDO
DA VINCI

Published by Oxford University Press, Inc.

LEONARDO DA VINCI

A Biography by
ELIZABETH RIPLEY

*With Drawings and
Paintings by Leonardo*

HENRY Z. WALCK, INCORPORATED

Distributors

1261

97
Leo

Copyright 1952

OXFORD UNIVERSITY PRESS, Inc.

ILLUSTRATIONS

LEONARDO
DA VINCI

ONE summer day in the year 1464 a handsome fair-haired boy of twelve was strolling along the slopes of a hillside in Italy. Below him the River Arno wound through the valley, a silver streak between the poplars lining its banks. He was carrying a sketch book and from time to time he would stop to sketch a flower or note the formation of a crag. Occasionally he paused on the crest of a slope and gazed above him at a bird circling in the sky and marvelled at its graceful flight.

The boy's name was Leonardo, and because he lived in the little village of Vinci, he was called Leonardo da Vinci. His father had a big law practice in the city which kept him so occupied that Leonardo was brought up by his grandmother. He seldom played with other children and cared little about school. He was happiest when alone, studying and sketching what he saw around him.

When Leonardo was sixteen he went to live in the city with his father, but he often returned to the country where he had lived as a boy to sketch and study nature. One summer day when Leonardo was a man of twenty-one he sat on his favorite slope overlooking the Arno valley and made a beautiful landscape drawing. When he looked at the finished sketch he was so pleased with the job he had done that he carefully dated the picture in the top corner: "Day of Saint Mary of the Snows, August 2, 1473," and in the lower right hand corner he proudly signed his name, "Leonardo."

THE ARNO VALLEY
Uffizi, Florence

When Leonardo was sixteen his father decided to bring his son to live with him in the city of Florence. He was so impressed by the drawings that Leonardo showed him that he sent the boy to study in the studio of the well-known painter, Verrochio.

Leonardo enjoyed the company of the other pupils. He was popular, because not only was he handsome and well-dressed, but he could sing and play the lyre. He was a superb horseman and so strong that he could bend horseshoes with his bare hands.

Although he took part in the gay life of the boys of his age, he spent most of his time alone. He loved to wander through the streets of the big city and sketch what he saw. He filled notebooks with pictures of buildings and people. He drew ugly old men with hooked noses and uncouth women with big teeth. The grotesque fascinated him as much as the beautiful. He wrote in his notebook:

"It is impossible to love or hate anything without first having cognizance of it."

CARICATURES
Royal Academy, Venice

Photo Anderson

At the time Leonardo came to live in Florence the city was ruled by a rich and powerful man named Lorenzo de Medici. One Sunday morning when Lorenzo and his brother were worshipping in the cathedral a man named Baroncelli tried to assassinate them. Lorenzo escaped but his brother was stabbed to death. Baroncelli was caught. Some months later a rope was put around his neck and he was thrown from a window of one of the palaces.

As the richly dressed body dangled wretchedly in view of the people of Florence, Leonardo, unmoved by the gruesome spectacle, stood in the crowd and sketched in pen and ink the hanging body.

In order to remember every detail of Baroncelli's clothing he made careful notes on the same page. He wrote his notes with his left hand so that they read backwards, as if they were held to a mirror. He noted the doublet of black satin, the long blue cloak lined with foxes breasts and the collar trimmed with black and red velvet.

After carefully recording the costume, Leonardo studied the assassin's face. He sketched it again in the lower left-hand corner. It does not look like the face of a murderer, but has an expression of gentle sympathy which appears many times in the faces painted by Leonardo.

BERNARDO BARONCELLI
HANGING
Musée Bonnat, Bayonne

Photo Giraudon

For several years Leonardo worked in Verrochio's studio. Florentines who visited the studio marvelled at Leonardo's talent. Soon he became known as one of the important painters of Florence. At this time the monks of the convent of Saint Donato were looking for an artist to paint an altarpiece, so they offered the commission to Leonardo.

The young artist started to work with enthusiasm. He chose as his subject the adoration of the kings. This was a favorite subject in Leonardo's time, for artists loved to paint the kings dressed in the rich costumes of the day. Leonardo, however, was not interested in painting a colorful pageant. To him the adoration of the kings was a miraculous incident filled with deep meaning.

In his notebook he described what he would paint.

"All those present at any remarkable happening," he wrote in his mirror writing, "look on at it with wonder in their faces . . . and if it is a sacred occurrence those who are standing round turn their gaze on it, giving various expressions to their adoration as though the host were being shown to them."

For days Leonardo sketched old men kneeling adoringly and young men with hands upraised in amazement. At the same time he became so fascinated planning an elaborate background for his figures that he completely forgot that he had promised to finish the picture at a certain date. The monks became impatient.

At last Leonardo transferred the drawing to the wall. The picture was still only in tones of gold and brown but the monks marvelled at what they saw. The Virgin and Child appeared like a calm island in a turbulent sea of worshippers. The background was a complicated arrangement of steps and intersecting arches.

The monks agreed that Leonardo had painted the groundwork for a masterpiece, but the painting never advanced beyond the brown and gold stage. The artist had worked so long on the picture that he had lost interest in it. In the meantime many of his fellow painters had left Florence which no longer seemed attractive to Leonardo, so, abandoning the altarpiece forever, he decided to seek work in Milan.

ADORATION OF THE MAGI
Uffizi, Florence

Photo Anderson

The city of Milan was ruled by a crafty and clever duke, Ludovico Sforza. He had a humped nose, cold eyes and small red lips. People called him Moro because his skin was dark like a Moor. He was greedy and pleasure seeking and prided himself on having the wealthiest court in Italy.

When Leonardo arrived in Milan he wrote a long letter to the Duke telling him in detail of all the things he could do. He described himself as a scientist, engineer and stage designer. At the very end of his letter he wrote that he could make paintings "to stand comparison with anyone else, be he who he may."

Ludovico, who entertained lavishly, soon called on Leonardo to design showy pageants at his court. One of Leonardo's pageants was a magnificient spectacle which he called the "Paradise Festival." When the curtain rose the audience saw before them a huge hemisphere of gold sprinkled with twinkling stars. Above it the twelve signs of the zodiac were outlined by flickering lights and the seven planets revolved in their orbits. As sweet music played singers floated by in flower-laden boats.

When Ludovico married Beatrice d'Este of Ferrara, he called on Leonardo to organize an extravagant display. The streets of Milan were decorated to receive the bride and other foreign guests. Famous swordsmen came from all parts of Italy to take part in a tourney which lasted for three days. Leonardo worked feverishly designing gorgeous costumes for the knights on horseback. When the great day came, spectators declared that Italy had rarely seen such colorful pageantry. The name of Leonardo was on everyone's lips and Ludovico was proud of the fame which had come to his court.

KNIGHT ON HORSEBACK
Windsor Collection, England

By gracious permission of H.M. The Queen

"I shall construct all sorts of things for purposes of attack and defense," Leonardo had written in his letter to Duke Ludovico. He described new and wonderful war machines which he was able to make. The Duke, who was carrying on a war against Venice, was very interested in Leonardo's designs.

Leonardo showed Moro a drawing of a chariot with scythes projecting from the wheels which would mow down the enemy on either side. On the same page he drew a picture of an armored car on wheels which looked like a tortoise. It was propelled by crank handles and is the first design ever made for a tank.

"I can make armored cars," he wrote, "safe and unassailable, which will enter the serried ranks of the enemy with their artillery and there is no company of men at arms so great that they will not break it."

Leonardo filled pages with plans for fortifications of Milan in case it should be attacked. But Ludovico lost interest in Leonardo's war machines. Perhaps he felt his ideas were too advanced. None of his designs was ever used.

Leonardo, too, became tired of creating instruments of war and turned once more to his painting. When he was offered a commission to paint another altarpiece, he accepted it gladly.

SCYTHED AND
ARMORED CAR
British Museum, London

British Museum Photo

The monks of the Church of the Immaculate Conception wrote a contract which said that the altarpiece for their new chapel "be painted in oil by the Florentine Maestro Leonardo." The painter was told exactly what to do. He was to show the Virgin and Child surrounded by angels and prophets. He was told what colors to use, how the garments should hang and the amount of gold brocade on each dress. The painting had to be finished on December 8, 1484.

Leonardo signed the contract and then quickly forgot its rules. He spent days wandering in the country seeking inspiration for his picture. He explored the mysterious darkness of grottos and woods. He contemplated the beauty and tenderness of a dim light with dissolving outlines. This was the atmosphere he would try to create in his picture.

After months of studying and sketching he started to paint. He showed the Virgin Mary kneeling in a mysteriously lit grotto. One protecting hand is held over the head of the Christ Child and the other hand rests on the shoulder of the young John the Baptist. Kneeling in the right corner is a beautiful angel who looks out at us from the picture and seems by her pointing hand to be telling the story of the painting.

Leonardo had bathed his figures in a magic shadow and light. He had created a painting of great tenderness and beauty, but he had not carried out one of the rules of the contract. For twenty years Leonardo tried to collect the money due him for his picture, but the monks refused to pay him as he had not finished the painting on time.

Although the Madonna of the Rocks did not satisfy the monks of the Immaculate Conception, today it is considered one of the world's great paintings.

MADONNA OF THE ROCKS
Louvre, Paris

Photo Alinari

When Leonardo arrived in Milan he knew that Ludovico was looking for a sculptor to design a statue of his father Francesco Sforza on horseback. In his letter to Moro Leonardo wrote:

"I can likewise undertake the execution of the bronze horse, which will be to the perpetual glory and immortal honor of my lord your father of happy memory and the illustrious house of Sforza."

After waiting for several years Ludovico finally gave Leonardo the commission to make the statue. He started to work with enthusiasm, planning the work with his usual thoroughness. First he sketched a rearing horse over a prostrate foe. Leonardo was a splendid rider himself and knew horses well. He spent hours sketching in the Sforza stables. Finally he decided a rearing horse would be too difficult to cast in bronze so he sketched a sedately pacing horse. After he had made sketches he set to work on a clay model.

When the model was finished it was placed in the courtyard of the castle for everyone to see. People held their breath in amazement. A poet wrote: "I firmly believe and am not mistaken that Greece and Rome never saw anything greater." Leonardo had expressed in this powerful horse and rider the true meaning of the name Sforza, which is the Italian for "force."

Ludovico marvelled and wrote to a friend: "There is only one man of merit, Leonardo the Florentine, who is casting in bronze the Duke Francesco."

But as Leonardo was planning the casting of the statue in bronze, Ludovico was anxiously defending Milan against the invading French king. The duke seized all available metal for guns and the bronze assigned to Leonardo was made into cannons. Ludovico spent so much money on armaments that he finally stopped payments to Leonardo.

In spite of Sforza's defense preparations, the enemy was too strong for him. The Milanese opened their gates and the French soldiers marched in. When they saw the statue which people had named "the Colossus," they threw stones at it to show their scorn of the house of Sforza. The great work crumbled to pieces.

Leonardo's beautiful drawings in pencil and India ink are all that remain to remind us of the Colossus.

SKETCHES FOR THE
SFORZA MONUMENT
Windsor Collection, England

By gracious permission of H.M. The Queen

While Leonardo was living in Milan a dreadful plague struck the city and many people died. In Leonardo's time cities were very dirty and germs spread rapidly. Leonardo, walking through the streets, was horrified at what he saw. Garbage was thrown out anywhere. There were no gutters with running water to carry away the refuse. The streets were narrow, crowded and poorly lit.

Leonardo dreamed of a city where these conditions would not exist. He drew a plan of a model town which had plenty of space and light. In his mirror writing he described the city in detail. No vehicles were allowed on the top level which was designed "exclusively for the use of gentlemen." On a lower level he planned a sewerage system where "privies, stables and other fetid matter must be emptied away underground. . . Let such a city be built near the sea or a large river in order that the dirt of the city may be carried off by water."

Hoping to improve conditions in Milan, Leonardo designed a new system of plumbing and drainage for the Sforza castle. When Leonardo's system was installed, Moro was delighted to find that it was clean and efficient. Leonardo, stage designer and sculptor for the House of Sforza, had proved himself also useful as an expert engineer.

DESIGN FOR
UNDERGROUND STREETS
Institut de France Mms.

Near the Sforza castle in Milan was the church of Santa Maria della Grazia where Ludovico used to worship. After mass he loved to walk in the quiet monastery garden which was connected with the church. Moro was grateful to the friendly silent monks for the peaceful hours spent in their garden. To show his appreciation he built a new dining room for the monastery. On the bare front wall he commissioned Leonardo to paint a picture of the Last Supper.

Leonardo was elated and plunged into the work feverishly. He would work far into the night and lie in bed late in the mornings, planning the painting in his mind. In order to force himself to get up, he invented a peculiar alarm clock. It was a contraption with pulleys attached to his bed which, at a certain hour in the morning, would raise his feet in the air.

As Leonardo composed the picture of the Last Supper in his mind, he wrote a detailed description of it in his notebook. He decided to paint the dramatic moment when Christ said to his twelve disciples, "One of you shall betray me." He made a sketch of the scene. Jesus is seated with eleven of his disciples at the far side of a long table. The traitor, Judas, is sitting alone at the near side. This composition was used by all Italian painters, but it did not seem to satisfy Leonardo. He decided to seat Judas among the other disciples and show by his expression and gestures that he was the betrayer of Christ.

STUDY FOR THE
LAST SUPPER
Venice Academy

Photo Alinari

For weeks Leonardo walked through the streets of Milan looking for a model for the head of Judas. He explored the slums, searching for evil-looking faces. Finally he brought to his studio a model with sharp features which he sketched in red chalk. There was no beard covering the pointed chin, but Leonardo added a beard in the final painting. With infinite care he chose eleven models for the other disciples and made beautiful sketches of each.

At last the final drawing was ready to put on the wall. Leonardo and his pupils climbed up on the scaffolding and began to paint. Ludovico used to visit the monastery often to see how the work was progressing. The monks, too, watched with interest. Leonardo was not disturbed by visitors. He even welcomed their criticism.

"Listen then with patience to the opinion of other people," he wrote, "reflect well on it and consider carefully whether the adverse critic is right in criticizing you. If you find that he is right, make good the error, if you do not find so, then act as if you had heard nothing."

The work progressed rapidly, but Leonardo still had not painted in the head of Christ. The monks waited and wondered while Leonardo searched Milan for the perfect face. At last he found the model he was seeking. He painted in the figure of Jesus framed by the bright light streaming in from the window behind him. The scaffolding was removed and the monks and Ludovico looked with wonder at Leonardo's masterpiece.

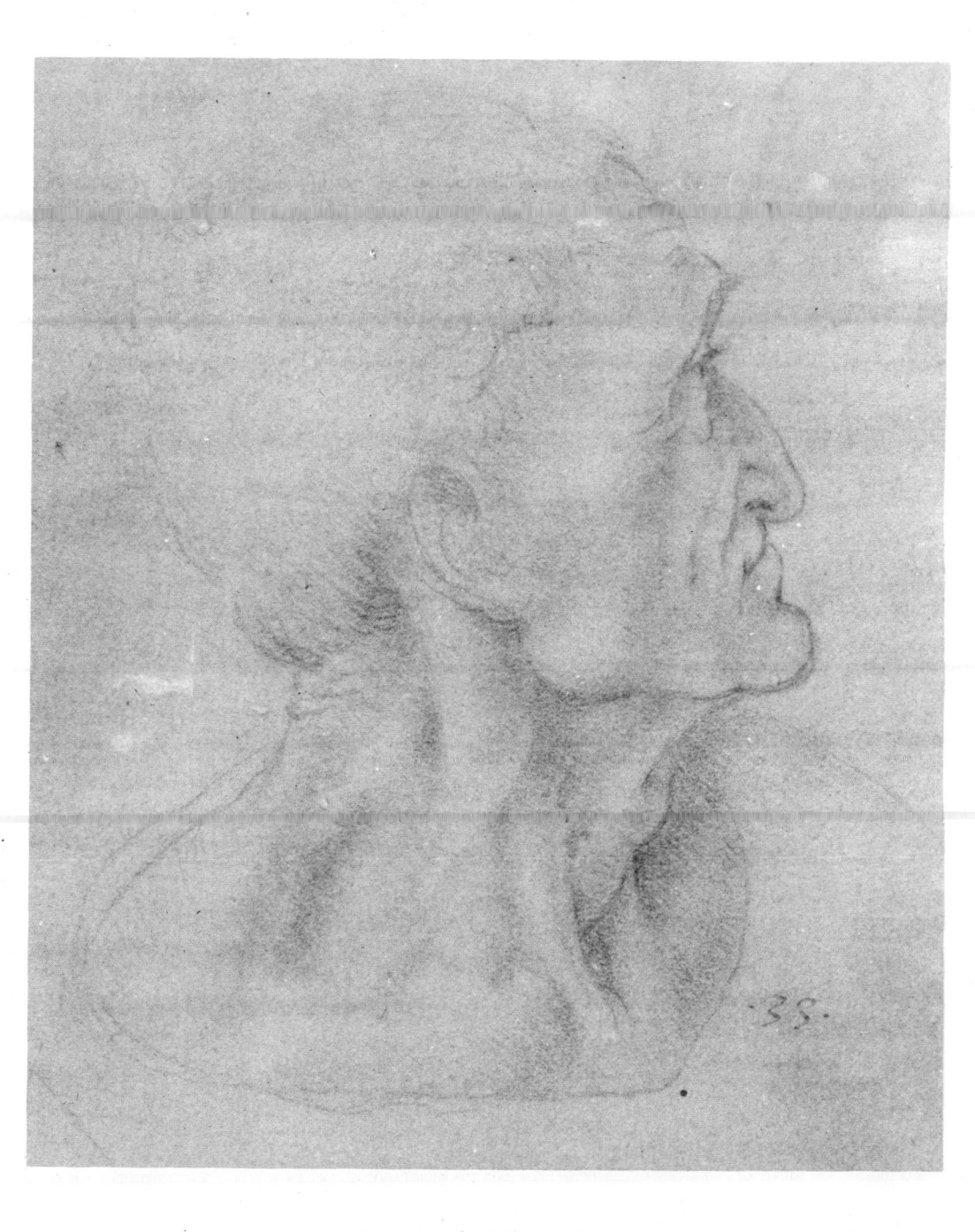

STUDY FOR THE
· HEAD OF JUDAS
Windsor Collection, England

By gracious permission of H.M. The Queen

Two years after Leonardo had completed the Last Supper the French king entered Milan. The conqueror was eager to see Milan's treasures, so very soon he went with his courtiers to look at Leonardo's painting. His enthusiasm was so great that he asked that, no matter what the cost, the painting be removed from the wall and taken to France. The king's wish could not be carried out, however, and the painting remained on the dining-room wall.

Unfortunately it did not remain there long. Only a few years after Leonardo had finished the Last Supper dampness began to seep through the monastery walls. The artist could see that the plaster on which he had painted his great picture was peeling away.

A beautiful shadow in faded colors is all that now remains of Leonardo's masterpiece.

THE LAST SUPPER
Santa Maria delle Grazia, Milan

Photo Anderson

Leonardo walked many miles looking for models for his Last Supper. He grew to know the city and the surrounding country well. He learned a great deal about the way people lived and worked. He watched men working with no machines to help them, and thought constantly of inventions which would save them time and labor.

He designed an efficient oil press to speed up the production of olive oil. The machine worked by a system of interlocking cogwheels. "I promise you," he wrote, "the olives will be pressed so thoroughly that they will be left almost dry."

The miracle of faultlessly interlocking cogwheels was fascinating to Leonardo. Using this effective gearing he invented many other labor-saving devices. As he watched cooks laboriously turning meat on a spit in front of a hot fire, he dreamed of a mechanical turnspit. He drew a picture which shows a small turbine wheel placed in a chimney. The heat of the fire set the wheel in motion and caused the cogwheels to rotate and the spit to turn evenly. "This," he declared, " is the right way to roast meat, because the joint turns slowly or quickly according as the fire is moderate or fierce."

Late into the night and during the long gray days of winter Leonardo experimented with his inventions. The weak flickering light of the oil lamp made work difficult, so he invented a lamp which would throw a bright light on his paper. He placed a wick in a glass cylinder filled with olive oil. He fitted the cylinder into a large globe of water. The glimmer of the burning wick was magnified many times by the reflection of the water. Leonardo's studio was flooded with a bright steady light. So pleased was Leonardo with his invention that he drew a picture of the lamp on a richly carved pedestal. Leonardo's design was used in Italy for over two hundred years.

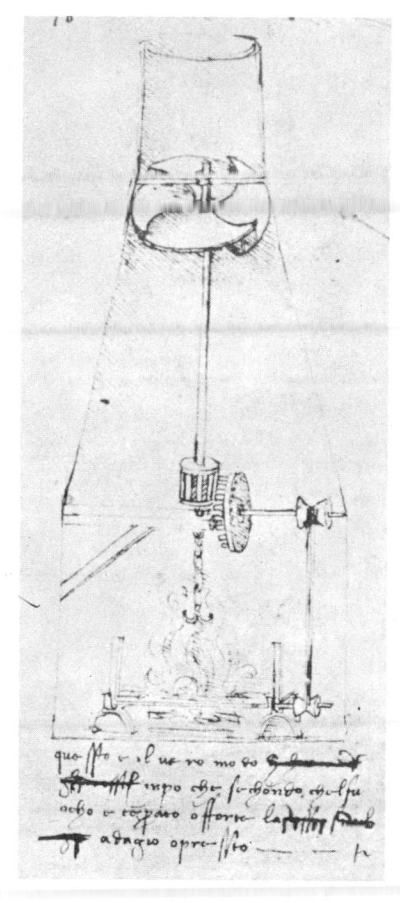

SELF-TURNING SPIT
Il Codice Atlantico

LAMP
Il Codice Atlantico

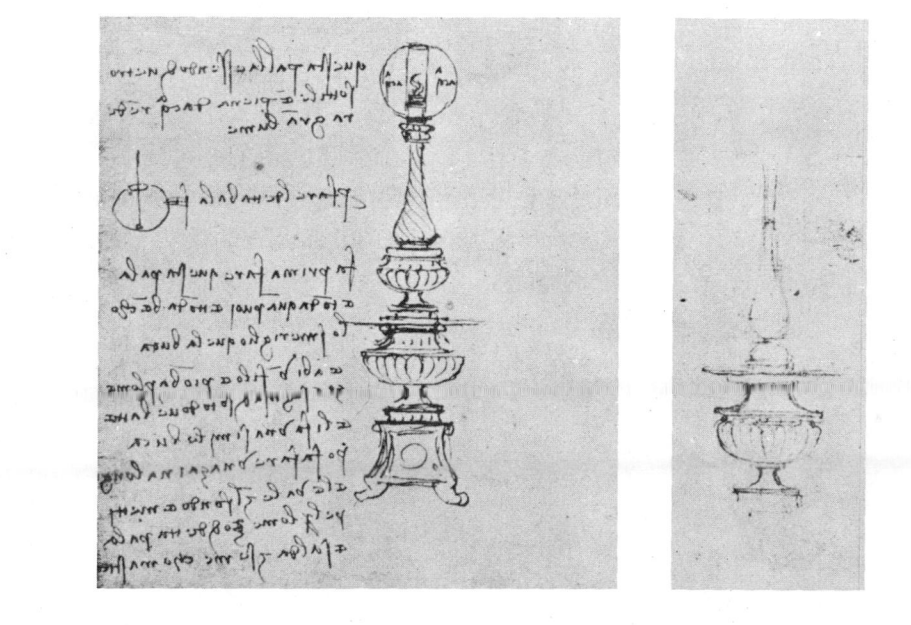

In 1499 Ludovico Sforza fled Milan before the conquering French king. Leonardo wrote in his diary: "The Duke has lost his kingdom, his possessions, his liberty, and all his works have come to naught." The man who had given Leonardo work for sixteen years was now in exile, and Leonardo would receive no more commissions in Milan. After putting his savings in a bank, he packed up his belongings and with his favorite pupil, set out for Mantua and the court of Isabella d'Este.

"The first lady of the world," one of Isabella's courtiers named her, for she was a brilliant and charming woman who had made her court the center of writers, artists and musicians. She was the sister of Beatrice d'Este, wife of Ludovico, and had often visited her sister in Milan. There she met Leonardo and admired his work. Many times she had written him begging him to paint her a picture and inviting him to her court. "Leonardo, the painter is our friend," she wrote.

So as a friend, Isabella welcomed Leonardo to Mantua. The artist to show his gratitude agreed to paint her portrait. As he sat before his model he saw a face of great intelligence and self-confidence. He sketched her in profile with her sensitive hands resting one on top of the other. Isabella would perhaps have preferred a more flattering portrait, but she was proud that at last the famed Leonardo was painting a picture for her.

As Leonardo was transferring the sketch to a canvas he was called to Venice on important business. Much to Isabella's disappointment he left the portrait unfinished. For years she continued to write him, begging him to finish the painting. His replies were brief —"Leonardo has nothing more to say," he wrote in answer to one of her letters.

Isabella treasured the charcoal sketch which Leonardo left in Mantua. But her blundering husband, Francesco Gonzaga, did not care for the cold unflattering picture of his wife and after a few years he gave the drawing away. Isabella never ceased to regret the loss of the picture, her only reminder of the great Leonardo's visit to Mantua.

ISABELLA D'ESTE
Louvre, Paris

Photo Giraudon

Leonardo arrived in Venice in March, 1500, to find the city humming with excitement. The Turks from the east were moving towards the city, burning and killing as they approached. The terrified Venetians were working desperately to build defenses.

When Leonardo, Italy's best known military engineer, arrived he was asked to make plans for the city's protection. He made a quick tour of the surrounding countryside, noting roads, rivers and valleys and reporting on the best way to defend them. He designed new cannon and supervised their construction.

While the Venetians worked frantically to carry out his plans, Leonardo one day informed the governors of the city that he had an invention which would deal a crushing blow to the Turkish fleet. He must have seemed like a magician to the Venetians when he described to them how, under water, they could approach and make holes in the enemy ships.

For many years Leonardo had been fascinated with the idea of man working under water. He had sketched a leather mouthpiece with a long breathing tube attached. He had designed a diving dress as "a means of escape in a tempest from a wreck at sea." The picture shows a man swimming in a belt filled with air and on the same page is a glove like a huge duck's foot to make swimming easier.

There are no pictures, however, of the diving dress he designed for the Venetians. He was careful to keep the plan as secret as possible. In his notebook he described in mirror writing how he would construct in his own house, with only a "simpleton" to help him, a diving dress made of armor plate. It would have a mask fitted with a glass plate and a tube for breathing attached to a bladder filled with air. The air supply would last for four hours and during this time the diver could bore holes in the biggest of the Turkish ships.

"I shall devastate the harbor!" wrote Leonardo in his report.

Perhaps the Venetians feared Leonardo's invention was black magic, or they may not have had the courage to try so daring a project. The under-water attack against the Turks was never made and Leonardo never mentioned the plan again. More than two hundred years passed before his dream of working under water was realized.

32

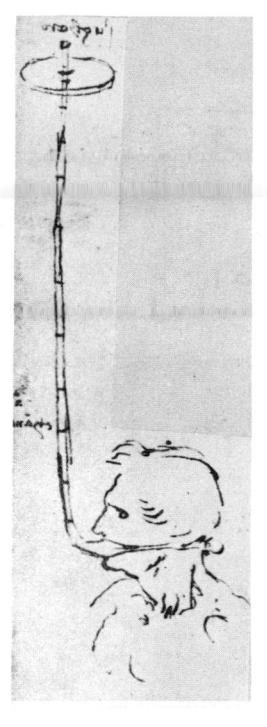

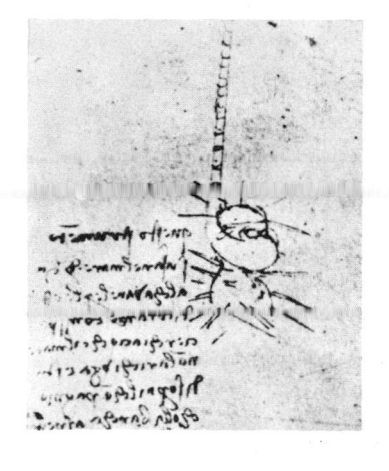

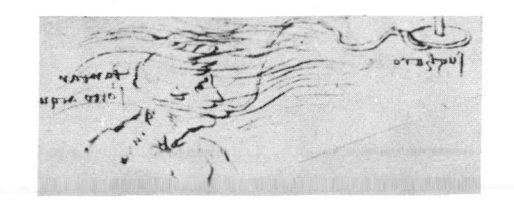

BREATHING TUBE
Il Codice Atlantico

BREATHING MASK
FOR DIVING
Institut de France

LEATHER MOUTHPIECE
Il Codice Atlantico

WEBBED GLOVE
FOR SWIMMING
and LIFE BELT
Institut de France

Leonardo did not remain long in Venice. Toward the end of April he decided to return to Florence which he had left sixteen years before. He was now forty-eight years old, but as handsome and strong as ever. His wavy hair and beard and carefully twisted mustache were still reddish blond. His penetrating blue eyes contrasted with his pink cheeks. He must have attracted attention as he wandered alone in the streets of Florence. He was perfectly groomed, but his clothes were strangely out of style. When men were wearing long full cloaks, Leonardo appeared in a short knee-length coat. He usually wore pink to make his fresh complexion look fresher.

For the past sixteen years the people of Florence had been hearing a great deal about the handsome and aloof artist who had designed the bronze horse and had painted the famous Last Supper. The Servite Monks were so eager to have the great Leonardo paint an altarpiece for them that they offered him board and lodging in the monastery while he was doing the work. Leonardo accepted the offer gladly, for he had not yet found a home in Florence. After an agreement with the monks had been signed, artist and pupil moved into the quiet seclusion of the monastery.

LEONARDO DA VINCI,
SELF-PORTRAIT
Windsor Collection, England

By gracious permission of H.M. The Queen

While the silent monks went about their duties, Leonardo shut the door of his cell and went to work. Completely forgetting the altarpiece, he opened up his books on geometry and became absorbed in a study which he described as a "sweet fruit . . . which nourishes the intellect." The monks tactfully reminded him that he had agreed to paint an altarpiece for their monastery. Leonardo, appearing not to hear their suggestions, calmly continued his studies. The hints at last became loud complaints which Leonardo could no longer ignore. Reluctantly he put aside his notebooks and began to plan the picture.

From Milan he had brought a drawing of the Virgin and Child with Saint Anne. This, he decided would be the subject of the altarpiece. As if he were still working on a geometry problem, he built the three figures into the shape of a tall pyramid. In order to fit the steep triangle in a narrow frame he had to place the Virgin on the lap of her mother Saint Anne. Such a daring composition had never been tried before, but Leonardo handled it so skillfully that the arrangement seemed quite natural.

At Easter time the drawing with its life-size figures was finished. The monks who had complained so loudly were now overwhelmed with wonder and pride. The gates of the monastery were left open for two days while the people of Florence filed by the masterpiece. Men, women and children believed the picture to be a miracle.

Only one man in Florence appeared to take no interest in the drawing. This was Leonardo himself. Ignoring the chorus of praise which echoed around him, he plunged once more into his studies of geometry.

VIRGIN AND SAINT ANNE
Louvre, Paris

Photo Alinari

"The excellent and most beloved servant, Architect and Engineer General, Leonardo da Vinci," wrote Duke Cesar Borgia, " . . . is commissioned by us to consider our places and fortresses in order that we may provide for them in accordance with . . . his judgment."

Leonardo had been appointed military engineer to the most cruel scheming adventurer of all Italy. The ambitious and ruthless Duke Cesar Borgia had murdered relatives and betrayed friends in his passionate desire for power. By intrigue and treachery he had taken possession of a large slice of northern Italy called Romagna. He saw himself ruler of a magnificient new kingdom. He planned to build a splendid capital city at Cesana, worthy of his name. He dreamed of a line of fortresses stretching from the city to the sea and he appointed Leonardo da Vinci, foremost architect and engineer of Italy, as the designer of his ambitious projects.

Cesar's Engineer General was given every help while planning these vast works. Every assistant was ordered to follow Leonardo's directions so as "not to incur our indignation." Leonardo first made a drawing of a castle for Cesana and on the same page rough sketches of a plan for the new city. Plots of ground were separated by streets which were numbered. He suggested building a canal to connect the capital with the seaport and drew plans for its construction.

During the spring and summer of 1502 Leonardo worked for Cesar. While the ruthless duke carried on his treacherous campaign, Leonardo drew military maps and even prepared a new blasting powder for him.

Never once did Leonardo mention Cesar's monstrous cruelty. He was not shocked to see man disobeying the laws of human justice. Only when man disregarded the laws of science did Leonardo record it in his notebook. He was so irritated to see the poorly designed four-wheel carts in the Romagna that he wrote of their "absurd construction," which placed the small wheels in front, thus throwing the weight forward and making progress difficult.

"The Romagna is the home of every sort of stupidity," Leonardo wrote indignantly at the end of his report.

38

STUDIES FOR HEAD OF
CESAR BORGIA
Royal Library, Turin

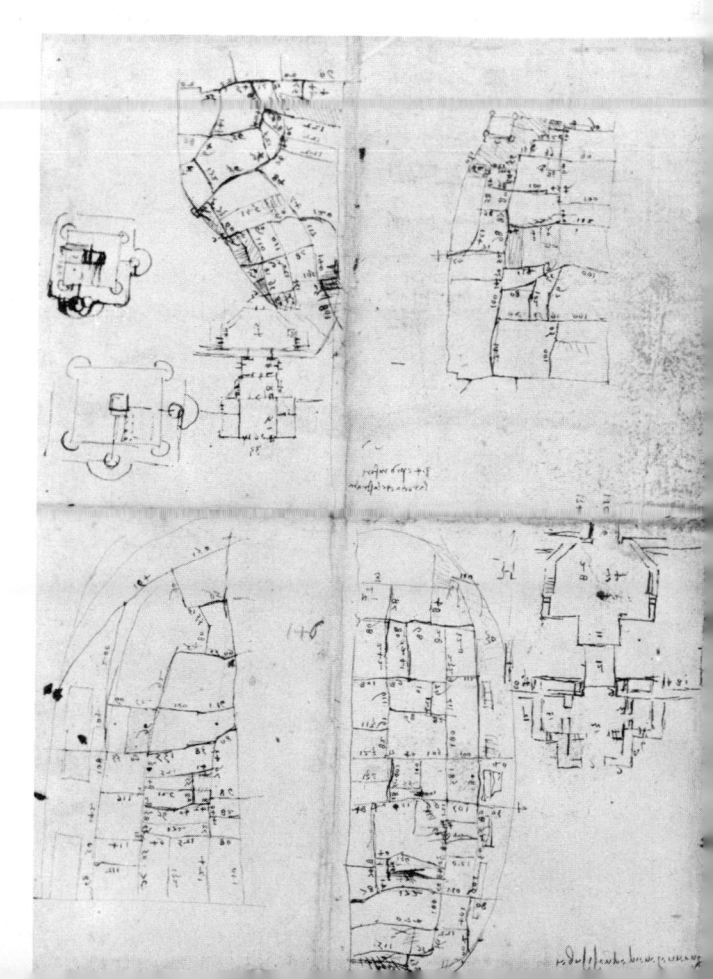

CASTLE AND PLOTS OF
GROUND PLAN OF CESANA
Windsor Collection, England

By gracious permission of H.M. The Queen

Cesar's kingdom did not last long. The duke was seized with a mysterious disease. People whispered that he had been poisoned. As he grew weaker he was unable to hold on to his power. Leonardo, whose services were no longer needed, decided to return to Florence.

Important changes had taken place in the city while Leonardo had been in Romagna. The last Medici ruler had died. Florence had become a free republic. The city council, eager to celebrate their independence, decided to decorate their chamber walls with scenes of Florentine history. When Leonardo applied for a commission it was instantly granted.

In the year 1440 Florence had defeated Milan in a bloody battle at a place called Anghiari. This was the subject Leonardo was told to paint on the council chamber wall.

"A battle," wrote Leonardo, "should be shown taking place amid clouds of dust and in the reflected light of a distant glow; it should be a maze of frenzied horses and fleeing men, a scene of horror . . . and do not leave any level spot that is not trampled and soaked with blood." This is how Leonardo planned to paint the wild fury of war.

He filled his sketch books with horses galloping, rearing and biting one another. Then he made drawings of strong men, stripped to show their powerful muscles. He placed the men on horses and plunged them into battle. He spent hours searching for the right models for the warriors' faces and when he found them he made drawings in red chalk.

Finally the city council, tired of waiting, ordered that a special scaffolding be made according to Leonardo's design. When the boards were pushed together it rose, and it sank when they were pulled apart. In the meantime Leonardo was experimenting with a new paint. He mixed his colors with wax which made them stick well to the wall. When Leonardo and his pupils mounted the scaffolding and started to paint they were delighted to find that the battle scene glowed brilliantly.

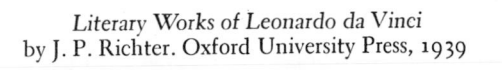

HEAD OF WARRIOR FOR
BATTLE OF ANGHIARI
Museum of Budapest

Literary Works of Leonardo da Vinci
by J. P. Richter. Oxford University Press, 1939

While the handsome well-groomed Leonardo was painting his battle scene, a tormented looking man in rumpled clothes, with a broken nose and dirty hands was furiously at work decorating the opposite wall of the council chamber. His name was Michelangelo Buonarti. Although several years younger than Leonardo, he had already become one of Florence's most popular artists. The city council had given him a commission to decorate one of the chamber walls and he had chosen as his subject another battle scene. In 1364 Florence was at war with Pisa. One day at a place called Cascina the Florentine soldiers were bathing peacefully in the River Arno when they were surprised by the Pisan soldiers. This was the scene Michelangelo had decided to paint.

The people of Florence watched fascinated as the cool restrained Leonardo worked on his scene of blood and fury, and the stormy Michelangelo painted magnificent nude figures in a peaceful setting. Artists travelled to Florence to give opinions on the two paintings. One autumn day a young art student named Raphael Sanzio came to watch the artists working. Without hesitation he chose the older painter's style as the one he would imitate, and he sketched two of Leonardo's horsemen in his notebook.

As the duel between the two painters continued, Leonardo noticed one day that the glowing wax colors were becoming dark as they dried. He mixed another solution of paint and proceeded to work on the bottom part of the picture. But the new mixture did not dry and after a few days it began to run in streaks down the wall. Leonardo and his pupils built a frame around the picture to hold the dripping paint, but still the color did not dry. Soon the Battle of Anghiari had vanished from the wall.

One hundred years later an art student from the Netherlands was travelling in Italy. In Florence he saw one of Leonardo's drawings for his battle scene. The central panel with its fierce tangle of horsemen fighting for the battle standard appealed to the energetic Peter Paul Rubens, and he made a copy in red chalk. This is all that remains of Leonardo's battle scene, for his drawing too has disappeared. Once more Leonardo faced bitter disappointment and the world had lost another masterpiece.

BATTLE OF CASCINA
BY MICHELANGELO
Holkam Hall, England

Collection of Earl of Leicester

RUBENS, DRAWING AFTER
LEONARDO'S BATTLE
OF ANGHIARI
Louvre, Paris

Photo Giraudon

Often while Leonardo was working on his furious battle scene he became obsessed by its violence. At these moments he would drop his work and return to the quiet of his studio. Here in the light of dusk, while musicians played soft music and a reader recited poetry, Leonardo painted the portrait of a young Florentine woman. She was the wife of a rich merchant named Giocondo, but she was usually called by her first name, Madonna Lisa or Mona Lisa for short. She was not beautiful, but she had an expression which fascinated Leonardo. As she sat calmly with folded hands and listened to the soft music a mysterious smile played around her eyes and mouth.

When Leonardo began the portrait, Mona Lisa was twenty-four, and she was thirty when the portrait was finished. Her face had grown broader and more placid, but her smile was as tantalizing as ever. Somewhere Leonardo must have seen this expression before, for the same smile flickers on the faces of Saint Anne and of the angel in the Madonna of the Rocks. Perhaps it was the knowing smile of Leonardo himself, for he wrote in his *Treatise on Painting* that the painter is so influenced by his own character that "it guides the painter's arm and makes him reproduce himself."

As a background for the reposeful figure of Mona Lisa, Leonardo painted a landscape of broken rocks and winding paths and streams which was bathed in a soft misty light.

"Let your shadings melt away like smoke, like the sounds of soft music," he wrote.

Leonardo came to treasure the portrait of the young woman which reminded him of the happy hours spent in her company. Not wishing to part with the picture he told Mona Lisa's husband that it was unfinished. He continued to work on the portrait for many years and even refused other commissions while he was painting it. Some years later the king of France, seeing the picture in Leonardo's studio, bought it from him. But as Leonardo could not bear to part with the picture, the king allowed the artist to keep it in his studio until he died.

MONA LISA
Louvre, Paris

Photo Alinari

Leonardo did not know that the Mona Lisa would become one of the famous portraits in the world. If he dreamed of fame he thought it would come because of his inventions. He believed that the invention which would bring him the greatest glory would be his flying machine.

Ever since he had been a boy, wandering on the hillside of Vinci, he had marvelled at the birds' flight. In Florence the bird sellers knew Leonardo well, for he used to visit them often and pay whatever price they asked for a caged bird. Then as the people in the market placed paused to watch, he would open the cage and let the bird fly up in the air. He did not hear the laughter of the crowd, for he was intent on studying the beat of the bird's wings. When he returned to his studio, Leonardo would write his observations in his notebook. He believed man would be able to fly if he had the proper wings, so he built two great wings of cloth stretched over ribs of wood. These he planned to attach to a man's shoulders. By moving his feet in a set of stirrups the flier would set the wings in motion.

DESIGN FOR WINGS OF
FLYING MACHINE
Institut de France Mms.

This was one of several designs which Leonardo made for a flying machine. Not one of them satisfied him. He drew a thick line through one of the drawings and started to work on an entirely new type. This was a sort of helicopter, which had two sets of wings attached to a post. The machine was worked by a man who stood in a kind of saucer and pedalled with his feet.

"You will test this instrument over water," he wrote, "so as to do yourself no harm if you fall." Leonardo thought a great deal about protecting the flier from crashes. "If a man have a tent roof . . . he will be able to let himself fall from any great height without danger to himself." The "tent roof" which Leonardo designed turned out to be a really workable parachute.

In the spring of 1505 Leonardo was invited to visit his uncle in the country. During the radiant spring days Leonardo would stand on the green hillside of Fiesole, looking up into the cloudless sky. As he watched the birds soaring in the air he dreamed of a still new type of flying machine. He decided that a man, equipped with wings, could be lifted from the ground by the force of the air, "like the bird of prey, the vulture, which I saw on my way to Fiesole," he wrote.

He designed a kind of glider, with wings like those of a bat. He planned to launch his machine from the Swan Mountain in Fiesole.

"The great bird will make its first flight—filling the whole world with amazement, filling all records with its fame, and bringing eternal glory to its birthplace." So wrote Leonardo as he pictured the first flight of the "great bird."

Did this flight ever take place? Leonardo never mentioned the "great bird" again. His flying machine did not bring him fame in his life time. Many years later the son of one of his friends wrote, "Leonardo da Vinci, also tried to fly, but he too failed. He was a magnificent painter."

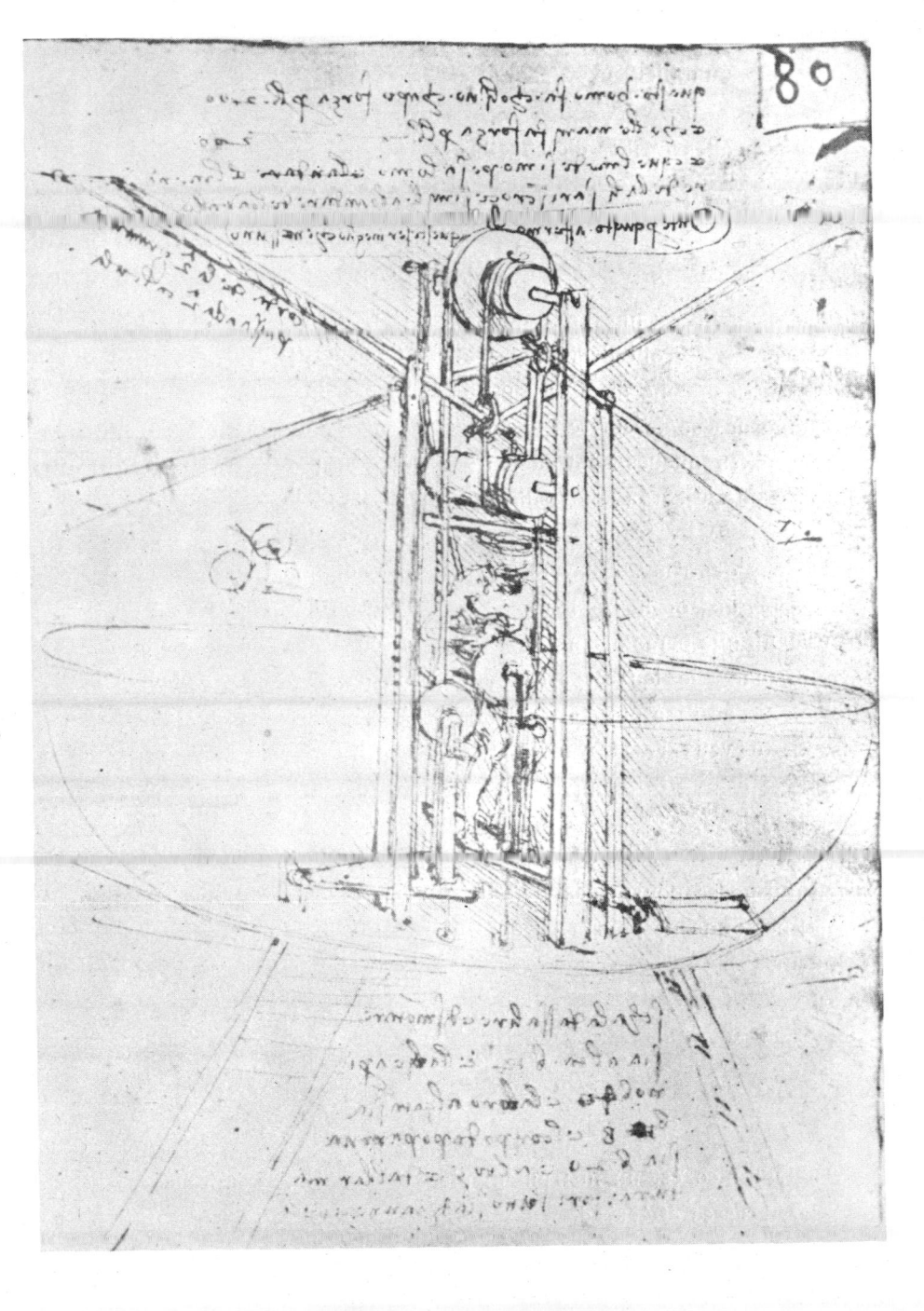

DESIGN FOR FLYING
MACHNE (HELICOPTER)
Institut de France Mms.

In the hospital of Santa Maria Novella in Florence an old man lay dying. Beside him sat Leonardo who listened sympathetically as the man told him in a weak voice that he had no pain but was very cold. Each day Leonardo returned to the dying man's bedside and watched him quietly, until finally the patient peacefully passed away. Leonardo wondered what could be the cause of "so gentle a death" and asked the monks of the hospital if he might dissect the body.

Alone in the ghostly light of the morgue, Leonardo examined the wasted muscles and hardened veins of the old body. In spite of the waves of sickness which overcame him, he continued his gruesome work. The study of the human body fascinated him. Leonardo had already begun a special notebook of anatomy. He had drawn beautiful muscles in action while he was painting the battle scene. Now, while dissecting the dead man's body, he hoped to find what made man live and die.

"I am revealing to men the origin of their being," he wrote, and again, "I want to work miracles."

While Leonardo was in Florence he dissected many bodies. He filled a whole notebook with beautiful drawings in red chalk. For the first time he mentions his ability in drawing. "If you are unable to draw, you will describe everything confusedly and convey little knowledge of the true forms of objects," he wrote in his anatomy book. He studied the position of the bones and where the muscles were attached. He drew the inside sections of a skull and made a careful drawing of the heart. "A wonderful instrument, the invention of the supreme master," he wrote under the picture.

As Leonardo examined the marvelous construction of the body he came to appreciate more and more how precious was human life. "Let not your rage or malice destroy life—for, indeed, he who does not value it does not himself deserve it!" So wrote Leonardo, and from that day till his death he never designed another war machine.

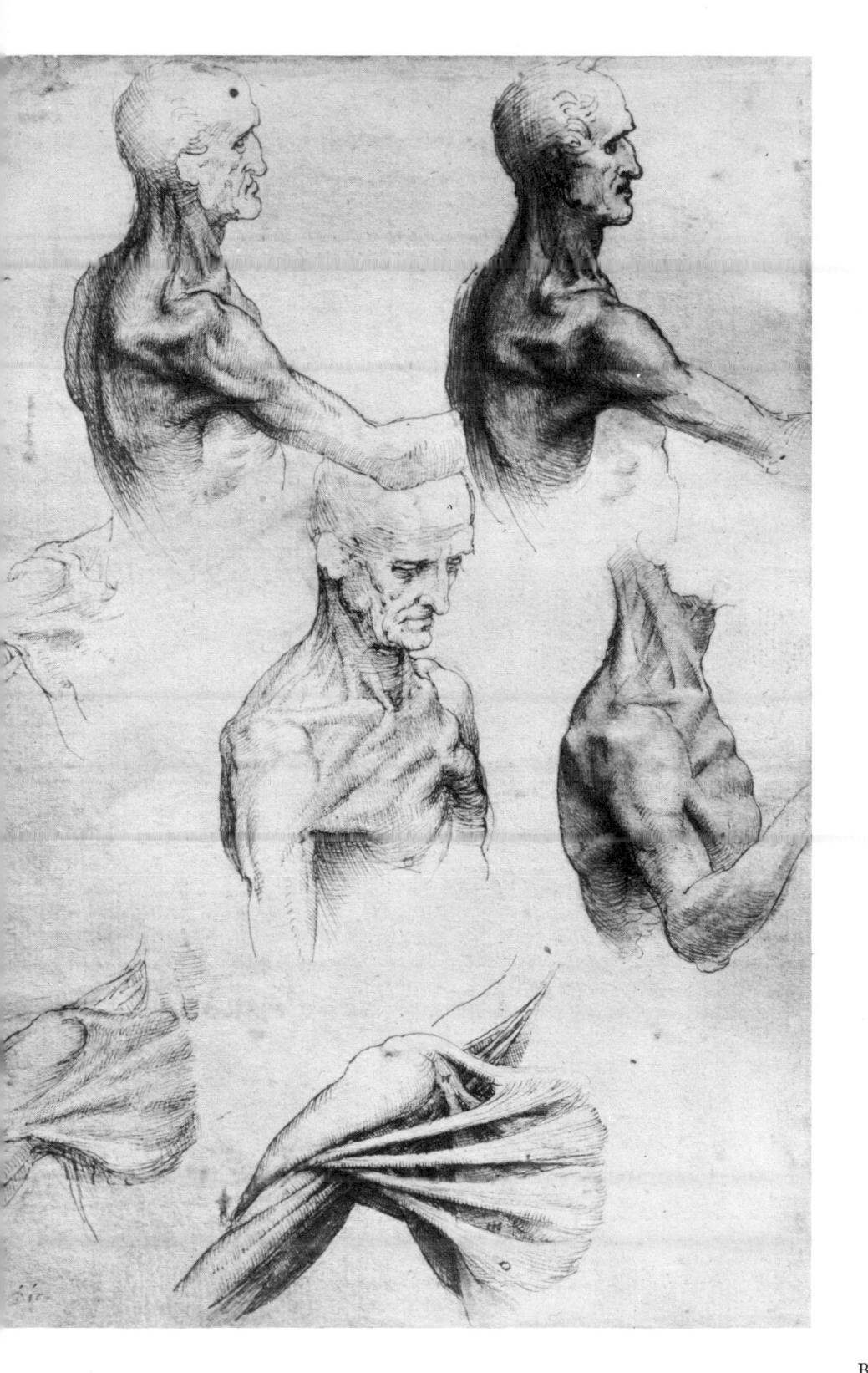

DRAWING OF THE
DELTOID MUSCLE
Windsor Collection, England

By gracious permission of H.M. The Queen

Leonardo arrived in Rome in the autumn of 1513. Leo X was Pope and his brother was the nervous sickly Cardinal Guiliano de Medici. He had known Leonardo in Florence and had admired his great genius. When he became Cardinal he summoned Leonardo to Rome. He offered him a generous salary, a beautiful home and a workshop. Never before had Leonardo lived so comfortably. A wing of the beautiful Belvedere Palace on the Vatican Hill was prepared for him. Partitions were put in, a kitchen installed and special furniture built.

Leonardo spent happy hours in the Pope's Botanical Gardens sketching rare and beautiful plants. He brought some of them to his studio and marvelled at the spiral arrangement of the leaves, which made it possible for each leaf to be exposed to the sun. He described in his notebook how a plant draws moisture from the earth. He discovered laws of botany which were not thought of again until one hundred and fifty years later.

Leonardo looked forward, however, to more important work which would bring him fame. Rome was the city of opportunity and he hoped to receive a big commission from the Pope. Leo X always gave a warm welcome to artists and scholars. Urged on by his brother the Cardinal, he soon asked Leonardo to paint a picture for him.

After waiting for some time, the Pope was told that Leonardo, instead of painting the picture, was experimenting with a new kind of varnish to use over the paint. Leo decided that this strange artist, who thought about the end before he began, could never accomplish anything and he lost interest in the painting. The picture was never painted, nor did the Pope ever ask Leonardo for another. His career as a painter in the court of the Pope had ended.

PLANT STUDIES
Windsor Collection, England

By gracious permission of H.M. The Queen

Leonardo did not win the fame he had hoped for in Rome. He saw younger painters receiving important commissions from the Pope. Michelangelo, who had painted the battle scene opposite Leonardo's, was at work on a gigantic tomb of Pope Julius II. The twenty-five-year-old Raphael, who had admired Leonardo's battle scene, was becoming rich and popular. Leonardo had to remind himself that fame did not depend upon material success.

"Beware lest greed for acquisition of gold stifle in thee love of art. Remember that the acquisition of fame is something greater than the fame of acquisition." So Leonardo comforted himself in his disappointment.

Ignored as a painter, Leonardo devoted his time to scientific studies. He plunged once more into his beloved geometry. He investigated the laws of gravity. Time after time he would climb a high tower and drop a weight from the top. The weight never landed directly below him, but always slightly to the east. From this he concluded that the earth turned on its axis.

Although the Pope did not appreciate Leonardo's genius as a painter, he did recognize his ability as a mechanical engineer. He asked Leonardo to design a minting machine which would make money for the Papal Treasury. Leonardo, never despising a job because it was too modest, went to work with enthusiasm. The machine which he designed "cut perfectly in roundness, size and weight." Instead of being made by hand, the coins now could be turned out rapidly so that, according to Leonardo the inventor, they could "pass only through the examiner and the stamper, and are especially fine."

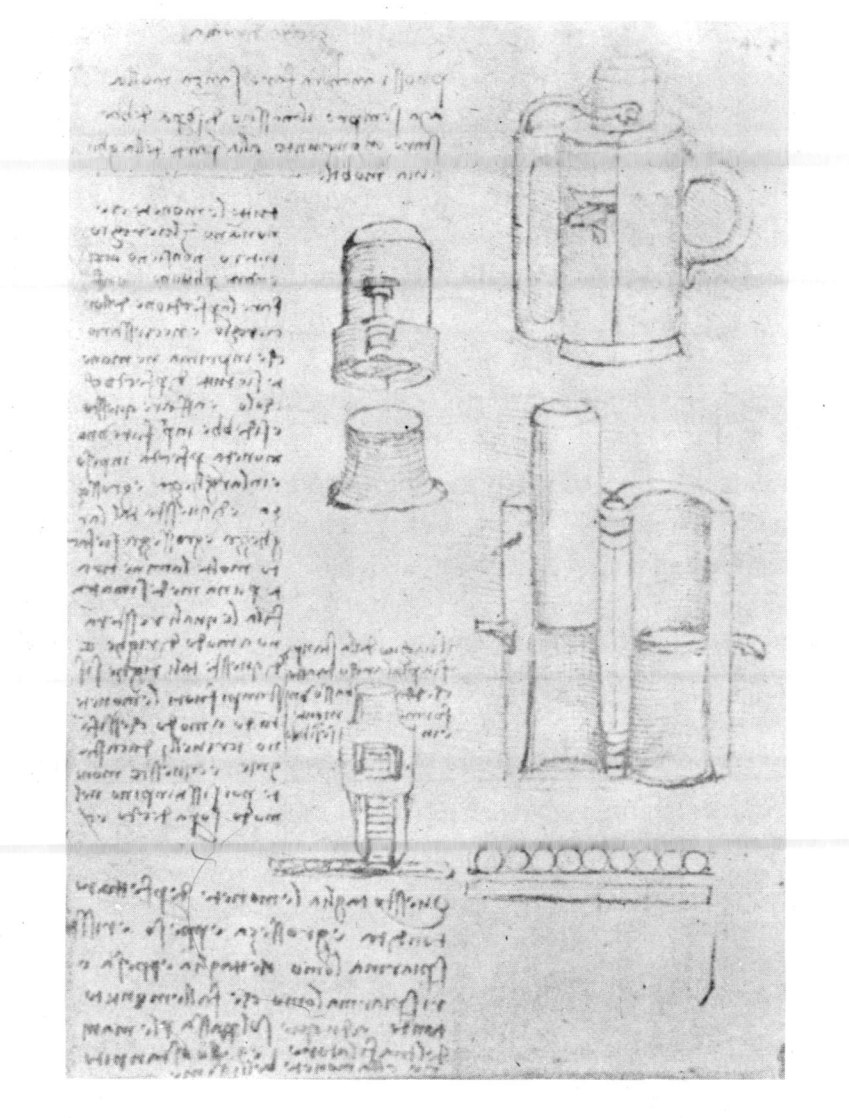

DRAWING OF MINTING
MACHINE
Institut de France Mms.

Leonardo was now over sixty years old. He had suffered many disappointments in Rome. Worn out by worries he fell ill. When he recovered he hurried to complete the many scientific studies which had begun, feeling for the first time that he might not have many years to live.

Once absorbed in his studies he became cheerful.

"Learning maketh the soul young, it decreaseth the bitterness of old age," he wrote. He took up the study of the movement of air and water, which had always interested him. He used to wander by the sea and watch the breaking waves. He would stand waiting for an approaching storm, studying the effects of wind, clouds and rain. What he saw he described in his notebooks. In the margins he made sketches of rhythmic eddies and swirls and of monstrous waves which formed themselves in geometric patterns. He imagined landscapes shaken by the fury of a storm. Then he pictured the whole earth wrecked by a hurricane. He made series of beautiful and exciting drawings called the "Deluge," which showed rushing waters and howling winds destroying the world. In this way, Leonardo believed, man would be punished for his sins.

Old and disappointed after years of waiting in Rome, the unhappy Leonardo dreamed of the end of the world.

DRAWING FOR THE DELUGE
Windsor Collection, England

By gracious permission of H.M. The Queen

In 1516 the large, resplendent army of Francis I, young king of France, swept down upon Milan and conquered the city. Triumphantly the conqueror returned to France and with him went his court painter, "Monsieur Lyonard de Vince."

Francis offered his court painter a generous salary and comfortable home. Although Leonardo was tired and sick he could not refuse the offer. His kind and faithful pupil, Francesco Melzi, helped him pack his belongings and in the company of the king's magnificent train they set out for France. Leonardo, who was sixty-four years old, would never see Italy again.

Francis I was gay. He loved pageants and fancy dress balls. Very soon after his return to France he asked Leonardo to stage festivals for him. When the king's baby son was christened at the Royal Castle of Amboise, there was a celebration which lasted for a week. There were fancy-dress balls at which Francis and his court danced far into the night. Leonardo made pictures of costumed figures for masquerades.

Then one morning the guests awoke to find that a fortress had been built in the castle square. From painted turrets wooden cannon fired hollow balls which bounced across the courtyard. Francis in shining gold armor led an attack on the fortress. The fighting appeared so real that one of the king's friends wrote: "It was the most splendid combat ever seen, and the nearest to actual war."

For the last time Leonardo had used his skill as a military engineer in this ingenious imitation of warfare.

MASQUERADE COSTUME
Windsor Collection, England

By gracious permission of H.M. The Queen

The castle of Cloux, which Francis I provided for Leonardo, stood on a small hill surrounded by trees. Looking over the tree tops Leonardo could see a little river flowing through the green countryside. Within walking distance, the king's castle of Amboise rose high above the River Loire. It looked like a fortress with its round towers and thick walls, but inside were gardens and buildings which reminded Leonardo of Italy. The French kings before Francis had imported Italian workmen to beautify the castle. But the new King Francis was more interested in making it comfortable. He called on Leonardo to help him.

Leonardo at once suggested changes which would make the castle safer. First the great ballrooms should be placed on the ground floor. "I have seen many rooms collapse and bury numbers of dead," Leonardo wrote.

He proposed methods of fire prevention and designed a system of ventilation which would carry off the smells which offended the sensitive Francis. Leonardo then suggested having a large inner courtyard with a pool where Francis could stage water tournaments.

Francis was so delighted with his new architect-engineer that he took him with him on his journeys from castle to castle. Leonardo was horrified to see the poor hovels which were provided for the nobles. He proposed a plan for making portable houses for them which could be taken apart and reassembled anywhere.

Riding over rutted roads was difficult for the aging Leonardo, so he suggested to Francis the construction of a water route which would connect his castles. He made plans for controlling floods and draining marshes.

Back and forth Leonardo travelled with Francis. The trips were exhausting. He had never completely recovered from his illness in Rome. He felt old and tired and longed to return to Amboise and settle peacefully in his little castle of Cloux.

SKETCH OF AMBOISE
Windsor Collection, England

By gracious permission of H.M. The Queen

On the whitewashed walls of Leonardo's castle of Cloux hung the pictures which he had brought with him from Italy. There were drawings for the Madonna of the Rocks and the Virgin and Saint Anne. The Mona Lisa was there too, for although Francis had bought it, he allowed Leonardo to keep it in his home.

In the studio of the castle at Cloux the aging Leonardo was painting a picture of Saint John the Baptist. He worked slowly for he was tired. He held his brush in his left hand for his right hand had been useless since his illness. As he had always written with his left hand he now found he could paint without too much difficulty.

He painted the half-length figure of the saint emerging from a shadowy background, as if lit by an unseen light. On the face is a beckoning smile. With one hand he points to a cross which can hardly be seen in his other hand, as if he were warning of approaching death.

This is the last picture Leonardo ever painted.

SAINT JOHN THE BAPTIST
Louvre, Paris

Photo Alinari

Early in the summer of 1518 quiet settled over the castle of Amboise. Francis and his gay court had departed. No longer would Leonardo be interrupted by daily visits from the restless energetic king, who used to pester him with questions on many subjects.

"No man ever born into the world knew as much as Leonardo," Francis once said. Patiently the handsome old man used to give out his great knowledge to the nervous king who hardly listened.

On June twenty-fourth Francis had departed and Leonardo sat at his desk and wrote in his diary, "Now I can go on." Although he was sixty-eight years old he had great plans for completing his many unfinished volumes.

"Life well spent is long," he wrote, but life seemed far too short to Leonardo for finishing all the work he had planned. Through the quiet summer days and the glowing warm autumn Leonardo worked undisturbed. Winter came with its fog and darkness. Winds blew around the castle of Cloux, and Leonardo, wrapped in his fur-lined cloak, felt cold and weak.

Spring came at last, but Leonardo no longer felt strong enough to work. Realizing that he did not have long to live he made preparations for his death. He dictated a will which was carefully worked out in every detail. To the faithful Francesco Melzi he left his books and paintings. To each of his servants he willed money or clothing. He gave careful instructions for his burial but no directions for a tombstone. The artist who had designed memorials for other men seemed to care little about his own.

On May 2, 1519, the devoted Francesco sat at his master's bedside. The artist silently gazed at the familiar face beside him. Then quietly Leonardo da Vinci closed his eyes for the last time.

Francis I, overcome with sorrow, wept when Francesco brought him the news of Leonardo's death. The young Francesco himself was overwhelmed with grief. Sad and alone he sat at his table and wrote a letter to his brothers in Florence telling them about his kind master's death. "To me he was like the best of fathers," wrote Francesco, "... It is a hurt to anyone to lose such a man, for nature cannot again produce his like."

64

SELF PORTRAIT (about 1510)
Turin Royal Library

Photo Anderson

ACKNOWLEDGMENTS

Most of the quotations in this book have been taken from the excellent biography of Leonardo da Vinci by Antonina Vallentin which was translated from the German by E. W. Dickes, Viking Press, 1938.

I wish to thank the Royal Librarian of Windsor Castle for giving me permission to reproduce six drawings from its collection; and Harcourt, Brace and Company, Inc. for permission to reproduce two drawing from *The Drawings of Leonardo da Vinci* with introduction and notes by A. E. Popham, copyright 1945 by Reynal and Hitchcock, Inc.

BIBLIOGRAPHY

Acher, Helen: *Five Sons of Italy*. Thomas Nelson and Sons, New York, 1950.

Clark, Kenneth: *Catalogue of Drawings of Leonardo Da Vinci at Windsor Castle.*

Coleman, Margeurite: *Amboise et Leonard De Vinci*. Arrault et Cie., Tours, 1932.

Il Codice Atlantico.

Institut de France Mms. Ravaisson-Mollien, Paris, 1881-91.

Lansing, Elizabeth: *Leonardo Master of the Renaissance*. The Thomas Y. Crowell Co., New York, 1942.

Lerman, Leo: *Leonardo Da Vinci*. Bobbs-Merrill Co., Indianapolis, 1940.

Lewis, Lorna: *Leonardo the Inventor*. Thomas Nelson and Sons, New York, 1948.

McCurdy, Edward: *Notebooks of Leonardo Da Vinci, Drawings of Leonardo Da Vinci.* Reynal and Hitchcock, New York, 1938.

Merejkowski, Dmitri: *The Romance of Leonardo Da Vinci.*

Reale Commissione Vinciana.

Richter, J. P.: *Literary Works of Leonardo Da Vinci*. Oxford University Press, 1939.

Taylor, Rachel A.: *Leonardo the Florentine*. Harper and Brothers, New York.

Vallentin, Antonina: *Leonardo Da Vinci*. The Viking Press, New York, 1938.